DIVORCED BUT NOT DEFEATED

Divorced But Not Defeated

Monica Tillett

ISBN: 9798991941402 (paper)
ISBN: 9798991941419 (ebook)

Cover design: Manzoor Ahmed

Printed in the United States

Published By: Monica L. Tillett

For questions, send written correspondence to: Monica L. Tillett at pursuit4greatness@gmail.com.

This book is dedicated to those who need the encouragement to move beyond their past and look toward their future.

Contents

Acknowledgments

I thank God for bringing the right people into my path to help me take a dream and make it a reality. The Lord nudged me to take Joshua Giles, "Write That Book Course," which encouraged me to start the writing process of this book, and the Lord kept nudging me along the way to keep going. Thank you Natalie for helping me proofread, and Andrea for your suggestions on the developmental editing. Thank you to my mom and Kimberly who helped me along that painful journey of divorce. I would also like to thank everyone who has supported and encouraged me during this exciting time of writing my first book. There will be more to come, in Jesus name!

Preface

Ever since I was a little girl I wanted to be married. I wanted to meet my prince charming, ride into the sunset, and have my happily ever after. I was a hopeless romantic. I loved being in love and wanted to be loved. Throughout high school and college, I dated and had some major love during that time. The problem was they either did not want to settle down and work towards marriage, or if they did, they were not faithful. I could not figure out why it was so hard to find the right man, fall in love, and get married. I mean, there was a happily ever after, right? Well at least that's what the romance industry said through the overwhelming number of movies and books they produced geared towards love. But with each failed relationship I found myself only wanting to find "the one" even more, and being heartbroken when it didn't work out.

Finally, one day, out of nowhere, I met my prince charming.

I met a man who was smart, intelligent, and good-looking. But most importantly, he wanted to settle down. He saw what he wanted and went for it, and that was incredibly attractive to me. He only knew me for a short time before he asked me to marry him. I could not believe it! All those years of dating men who never wanted to settle down, and then when I wasn't even looking for a relationship, was a man who wanted to get married. I had just ended a relationship and had no interest at that time in getting into another one. But here was this man, who kept trying to get my attention as I drove by his apartment each day. "Who is this man?" I would ask myself. Then one day, as he was trying to get my attention, as he usually did, I stopped to speak to him. He was very nice, could carry an interesting conversation, and had a great sense of humor. I thought to myself, "Ok, this is nice." As quickly as I met him was as quickly as we got married. I did not take much time to seek God to determine if this was who He had for me, because I was so caught up in my feelings. I called myself praying and seeking God, but if I was really honest, I had already decided in my heart what I was going to do. So, I had convinced myself that what I wanted was what God wanted too...even though I never received confirmation from God. It was my free will that overpowered the voice of God.

I decided to move forward with marriage. Again, thinking that once I said, "I do," I would ride into the sunset with my prince charming and live happily ever after. We got married at the Justice of the Peace, and so the journey began....

This is not just another book about love, marriage, divorce, and picking up the pieces. The Lord prompted me to write this book to focus on the process of His redemption and restoration as it relates to divorce. He wanted me to share my experience to help others who may be feeling that God does not love them, or that they have committed an unforgivable sin by getting a divorce. Unfortunately, some of the Church have made people feel that divorce is unredemptive. God wanted me to tell you of His love, and that He can redeem anyone and any situation. I pray you feel the power of God and see His love as you read this book.

Introduction

Society has created a standard that says you are successful if you are married and have children. But what happens when your life is different? If you're married, it's not good enough unless you have children. Or if you have children, it's not good enough unless you're married. Then if you're married and have children, it's not good enough unless you own your own home. The list goes on and on. Nothing is ever good enough. There is always another standard to try and achieve. But just when you think you've mastered explaining why your life may not look as society expects- a divorce happens! Now you not only have to deal with the hurt and flood of feelings that go along with it, but you also have to deal with explaining *why* you got a divorce.

Assumptions and accusations begin, followed by opinions on what you should have done. Everyone has an opinion. Before I got divorced.... *I had an opinion.* I remember discussing with my brother how I was feeling about getting a divorce, and how I felt judged. He confessed to me that when he was going through his divorce that I had made him feel judged. I didn't realize how it felt, or how easy it was to push my opinions onto him about how things should have been different. I didn't fully realize it until I had experienced it myself.

The emotional overstimulation is constant. You are constantly answering questions on why your marriage ended, while battling within yourself thoughts on what you may have done wrong to make your spouse want to divorce you. You may have even experienced losing some friends, or even having to switch churches. And to top it off, on any form you fill out, you have to answer the question if you're- single, married, divorced, or widowed. I understand there are situations where this is necessary to know, such as buying or selling real estate, medical procedures, and financial transactions. *But is it really needed for everything?*

I'm sure there are many of you with similar stories. I only wanted to illustrate how everyday encounters can begin to shape how people begin to view themselves and their situations. Depending on the type of encounters you have with other people, certain situations, and even your spouse, can begin to shape feelings of self-doubt, shame, and guilt.

In this book, you will learn that divorce does not mean failure. You will also gain strategies on how to build a positive self-image and gain the confidence to move forward despite other people's opinions. In fact, you will be able to gain insights into how to create a better future during your time of singleness. You will also learn techniques to combat self-doubt, guilt, and shame associated with divorce. Most importantly, you will learn God's love for you and how to allow Him to direct you towards a hopeful future.

This book is not a "tell-all" book about my divorce, nor is it meant to point blame. So, if you are looking for dirt or drama- go watch the soap operas! However, I will tell you that I was married for 12 years and tried extremely hard to make things work to the point where self-perception and self-blame became very unhealthy. I wanted to help others who may have experienced this. I was prompted by the Holy Spirit to write this book to show how His Light can shine through even in dark situations. And let me say this...... I do not regret this road. It was a challenging road that seemed dark and scary at first, with many lessons learned along the way. But what seemed to be my biggest, darkest battle, God turned and used it for my good. He can turn any situation around for your good, too.

"And we know that God causes everything to work together for the good of those who love God and are called according to his purpose for them." Romans 8:28 NLT

1

The Naked Truth

"Everyone then who hears these words of mine and does them will be like a wise man who built his house on the rock. And the rain fell, and the floods came, and the winds blew and beat on that house, but it did not fall, because it had been founded on the rock. And everyone who hears these words of mine and does not do them will be like a foolish man who built his house on the sand. And the rain fell, and the floods came, and the winds blew and beat against that house, and it fell, and great was the fall of it."
Matthew 7:24-27 ESV

Before we begin, let's ponder these two questions:
1) Is marriage something you can prepare for?
2) Is divorce avoidable?

Whoa! Two very loaded questions with many interesting answers! I believe that in everything, the best decision is made when you can count the cost. Look at all the possible outcomes before making a decision. There are so many scenarios on how to avoid the "shoulda, coulda, woulda's." When it comes to divorce, we often ask ourselves, "What could I have done differently?" The truth is, there are times when we could have done things differently, and then there are times when some things are out of our control. I fell in love and got married quickly without counting all the costs. In my mind things were going to work out, and I determined I would do everything possible to make that happen. I never considered that it wouldn't work out. Addressing problems in a marriage takes committed effort on both parts, and even then there could be other reasons hindering the marriage. Hindsight is helpful in determining possible changes that could have been made; however, this chapter looks at some crucial things that I realized I could have done differently from the beginning.

In order to make an accurate assessment of a situation, you have to look at the truth. The naked truth, without sugar coating, can reveal many things. We may not like what it reveals, but true growth and understanding lies in the truth. The truth does not change, it always remains the same. Take a moment to sit and reflect on who you are now, and compare yourself to who you were then. When I reflected on myself these were the things that stood out to me as far as what I could have done differently: preparation, direction, and priorities. They say hindsight is 20/20 right? Let's look at these a little closer.

Preparation

Be Intentional

I now realize that I was not ready to get married. I had no true perception of the responsibilities of a wife or husband. What does it mean to be a wife or a husband? And how do you prepare for that? Those are two questions that should be considered before getting married. Watching romance movies and hoping to meet prince-charming doesn't cut it. Reading books on marriage, or even consulting with your pastor, or trusted friends and family members who have been married are great starts. But don't just read *anything*, or talk with *anyone*. Be intentional. Look at the fruits of that marriage. What does that marriage look like? How do you see each spouse treating each other? Granted, no one knows what is going on behind closed doors, and no marriage is perfect, but even the Bible tells us that we can judge some things by what we see. This is different than making assumptions, because you are judging the actions instead of assuming what the actions would be. For example, Matthew 7:17-18 states, "A good tree produces good fruit, and a bad tree produces bad fruit. A good tree can't produce bad fruit, and a bad tree can't produce good fruit." Working in healthcare I meet a lot of people. People who have been married for 30+ years. I like to watch how they treat each other. I see some spouses making every effort to help the other spouse even if they are physically unable to. They would take their last step and give their last breath to make sure that spouse had what they needed. On the other hand, I've had spouses tell me directly that their spouse was going to need to find someone else to help them, because they were not going to do it. And frankly, there were some situations I've been in with spouses that made me really uncomfortable. While it's not my job to judge them, or their marriage, if I wanted to hear some helpful advice on how to have a good marriage then I would be more likely to ask the first couple.

I remember asking a close Christian friend before I got married for any advice she may have for me. I remember her saying, "Make sure you see them in all their seasons." Meaning, you need to see how they act when they are angry, happy, sad….you get the point. Once you can see their temperament during these different times, then you can determine if they are someone you are willing to deal with. When you are in a rush, it's hard to really see all of those seasons. Of course everyone has bad days, but a consistent performance is a pattern. So, keeping an eye on unhealthy patterns is when you should consider it a red flag. Take the time to slow down. Love is exciting, but take the time to pray, seek wisdom, and observe.

What have you taken the time to see? Were there any red flags or concerns that stood out to you? Take note of these things in the *Self-Reflection Journal* at the end of the chapter. You will need them as you prepare for the future.

Seeking Godly Attributes

We all have our list. You know.... the list of what we want in our ideal spouse. I didn't feel like my list was unreasonable. I wanted an attractive man with a great personality, who was a hard worker and able to provide for our family. Most importantly, I wanted someone who truly loved me. While all those attributes were good, there was more I should have been looking for.

Now, let's dive deeper into the attributes of a wife and husband as outlined in the Bible. Reading through these attributes can assist you in knowing what to look for in a future spouse. These characteristics were taken from Proverbs 31:10-29 and Ephesians 5:21-33 NLT.

Characteristics of a wife:

- Virtuous (high moral standards), capable, and precious
- Can be trusted and enriches her husband's life
- Brings good and not harm
- Works hard, gets up early, and directs the inner workings of the household
- Woman of business
- Energetic and strong
- Good steward of what she has been entrusted with
- Helps others
- Prepared
- Takes pride in her appearance
- Well-respected
- Confident
- Wise
- Give instructions with kindness
- Carefully watches everything in her household
- Fears the Lord
- Submits to her husband

- Respects her husband

Characteristics of a husband:

- Has a good reputation in the community and able to sit in a place of leadership
- Submits to his wife out of reverence to Christ
- Loves his wife as Christ loves the church
- Loves his wife as he loves himself- meaning he cherishes her and treats her well

Ephesians 5:22-28 MSG describes it like this: "Wives, understand and support your husbands in ways that show your support for Christ. The husband provides leadership to his wife the way Christ does to his church, not by domineering but by cherishing. So just as the church submits to Christ as he exercises such leadership, wives should likewise submit to their husbands. Husbands, go all out in your love for your wives, exactly as Christ did for the church-a love marked by giving, not getting. Christ's love makes the church whole. His words evoke her beauty. Everything he does and says is designed to bring the best out of her, dressing her in dazzling white silk, radiant with holiness. And that is how husbands out to love their wives. They're really doing themselves a favor-since they're already 'one' in marriage."

When I read this particular passage in the MSG Bible I couldn't help but say, "Yes! That's what I'm looking for!" Such a clear picture came to mind! These scriptures did an excellent job describing some of the attributes of a wife and husband. Your spouse could have all the money in the world, and buy you the most expensive things, but if they don't know how to cherish or respect you, what good are all the material things? Are these the only attributes you should look for? Of course not, but they are a good start. Consider your values, beliefs, and other things that are important to you and add those to the list too. Once you outline what's important to you, you can determine what you will and will not accept before entering into marriage.

I feel these attributes are important for both husbands and wives to demonstrate. For example, it's important for the husband to give instructions with kindness and to be a good steward of what he has been entrusted with, not just the wife. Again, decide what attributes are important to you. Once you know, then you know who you want to give entrance into your life. Needless to say, I have since made a new list.

Direction

Have you ever driven to a new place without first looking at directions on how to get there? I know we now live in a time where all we have to do is type the address or location into Google or MapQuest and we instantly get directions. I remember when I first started driving, I kept a small map in my car just in case I got lost. But thank the Lord for new technology that makes getting to places easier! I tried looking at a map the other day and just shook my head. It was so hard to understand! The point is- we don't just drive blindly when we have somewhere specific we need to go. Now, random sightseeing to pass the time is different, but when there is no time to waste, you need specific instructions to get where you need to be. Here are some simple steps you can take to assist with seeking God during this process:

Pray

Begin by praying. Let God know your desire to get married. Ask Him to show you how to prepare, what to look for, and to send the right person your way. It's simply just starting the conversation with Him in order to let Him know you want His help on the process.

Great advice, right? Only I did not do this, and it was such a huge mistake on my part! Looking back in hindsight, I see this was the first mistake. When I did not take the time to properly seek God and what His Will was for my life was like me saying, *"I got this."* I was giving a non-verbal message to God that said I could do it on my own. Had I even taken the least amount of time to seek wisdom and direction from my pastor or others instead of using my feelings as direction I would have seen my inadequate preparation and lack of direction. The surprising thing was that all of this was against who I was as a person. Everyone who knows me knows I am a person with well-thought-out tendencies. I never do things on a whim. I think, prepare, *then do.* But I was too quick and didn't take time to seek God's direction.

Identify your vision and direction

Before bringing someone else into your life, you much first determine what your vision and direction is. If you don't know which direction you are going, it will be easy to get off track when someone else comes into the picture. Where do you see yourself going? What do you want to accomplish in life? How will your vision and direction be affected when you get married?

For example, I knew I wanted to be a physical therapist since I was a junior in high school. Once I determined that, I set my plans to attend college to take the classes needed to prepare. Despite different set-backs, I continued to press forward toward my goal of becoming a physical therapist. Getting married did not affect this goal. Your God-Given Helpmate will only enhance your ability to achieve your goals, not subtract from it.

Determine your values and beliefs

I can not stress how important this is! Determining your values and beliefs are critical to your success as an individual. They shape your character and attract like-minded individuals. We have to know what we want, and don't want, in order to establish healthy meaningful relationships. When we compromise our values and beliefs to accommodate those who we want in our lives, we are putting their values and beliefs above ours which can result in compromising who we are as a person. According to *Pediaa.com*, "Values are principles or standards of behavior that is considered valuable or important. Values shape an individual's character and behavior; they are the basic foundation for a person's personality, behavior, attitudes, and perceptions. We always make decisions about right and wrong based on our values. Belief is a conviction that we generally accept to be true, especially without actual evidence or proof. They are the assumptions we have about the world, and our values, attitudes, and behavior are greatly influenced by these beliefs[1]."

As you can see, if you don't know what values and beliefs shape your decisions, then adding someone into the intricate parts of your life, such as a spouse, can create havoc if not chosen carefully. The Bible tells us in 2 Corinthians 6:14, "Do not be unequally yoked." This verse isn't meant to isolate you from others in a way that makes you superior to them. No, it simply means that when you spend time with those who think and believe differently than you, then there will eventually come a time when you will disagree on direction because your views will be different.

What are some of your values and beliefs? Jot them down in the **Self-Reflection Journal** at the end of the chapter.

Priorities

When you do not take the time to put God first you will struggle with keeping God first. Another personal mistake of mine. It seemed I was in a constant struggle of knowing who to put first- God or my husband. Had I taken the time to prepare myself for marriage, affirm my values and beliefs, and determine my non-negotiables, I do not feel I would have had as much difficulty knowing what to do in certain situations.

But as stated in the earlier sections, when you do not determine what direction and values are important to you, it will be easy to compromise your standards in order to make others happy. I did not know how to properly be a wife and stand firm on my beliefs, which resulted in me putting my husband before God and compromising on things in which I knew better. I struggled between being submitted to God versus being submitted to my husband. Here's a good example of what I'm talking about. Paying my tithes was very important to me. It was a value that had been established in me through my parents and Christian upbringing. I knew the importance of honoring God with a tenth of my income. See Malachi 3:10. This was something we had discussed prior to marriage, and something that was agreed upon. However, there came a time when we disagreed on whether we should continue to pay tithes. This was very upsetting to me, because it was very important for me to be obedient to God and submissive to my husband. So, to keep the peace, I agreed and stopped paying my tithes even though I knew it went against what was important to me. In this situation, I put my husband's desire above my desire to be obedient to God. In hindsight, I should have chosen a different response, but it taught me a valuable lesson in standing firm in my values, beliefs, and priorities.

This brings us back to the foundational verse for this chapter.

"Everyone then who hears these words of mine and does them will be like a wise man who built his house on the rock. And the rain fell, and the floods came, and the winds blew and beat on that house, but it did not fall, because it had been founded on the rock. And everyone who hears these words of mine and does not do them will be like a foolish man who built his house on the sand. And the rain fell, and the floods came, and the winds blew and beat against that house, and it fell, and great was the fall of it." (Matthew 7:24-27 ESV)

When the marriage is built on Christ your foundation will hold firm. But when you allow other people or things to come between you and Christ, things will in time fall apart. If I had taken the time to truly seek God before getting married, understand the attributes of a wife and husband, and understand that getting married shouldn't disrupt my relationship with God, then I would have not struggled as much in certain situations. Being impulsive and acting on my own told God I didn't need him, and so the problems that came with the marriage were a result of my pride.

Pride.....that was really the underlying problem. A problem that I'm now allowing God to deal with at the age of 42. I actually feel very ashamed when I look back at the course of my life and see how pride has affected so many areas-my relationship with God, my marriage, and my career. But I'm glad to say that I am now allowing God to work in me. Every day is a work in progress, and I still have a lot of growing to do, but God is helping me remove the areas of pride and replace them with humility. In fact, as I am writing this book, I am continually seeking God for His words and not mine, which says, *"You lead me Lord."* He put this book in my heart to share with others. Believe me when I first thought about writing this book shortly after I got divorced, it would have gone in a whole different direction! I thank God for changing my heart and the direction of this book so He can be glorified.

Now you may notice that I am mostly highlighting my own short-comings; although, I may at times reveal certain situations to help bring clarity to a point. God led me in this direction in order for Him to be glorified. If I chose to use the blame game, then the focus would have been taken off of God, which would have defeated the entire purpose of this book. In order to heal and grow, I had to reflect upon my mistakes. I cannot focus on what my ex did wrong. I will, however, focus on what God has revealed concerning the attributes of a husband and decide not to settle for anything less than that in the future. As well as, how to stand firm in my values and beliefs.

Remember, God is able to pull us back to him, and He can use any situation to do it. I want to highlight the process I went through as I went from being married to being divorced and how I see God's hand and love with me throughout the journey. Look at what Jesus told Simon in Luke 22:31-32 ESV:

"Simon, Simon, behold, Satan demanded to have you, that he might sift you like wheat, but I have prayed for you that your faith may not fail. And when you have turned again, strengthen your brothers."

The devil wanted this divorce to be devastating emotionally, spiritually, and in some cases physically. The devil wanted me to be so cast down that I forgot God and deviated away from God's will for my life. But I thank God that Jesus prayed for me. I didn't know it at that time, but now as I look back, I see that because Jesus prayed for me, I was able to pull through and now turn around to help someone else. It's funny that when I submitted this book to an editor for developmental editing, meaning they look for ways to add to the manuscript to make it better, she kept saying I needed to have facts- that people can't just take my word for it. She also said that the topic of divorce has been written about at nauseum, and to look for an angle that made this book different and relevant now. I tried changing some things, and God allowed those changes, but most of it He wanted me to keep the same. Why? Because people need to know who God is in all situations, not who we have been taught He is by religious rules. There are people going through the same thing and God has told me to turn around and help my brothers and sisters so that they can be free too. What makes it fact, is that I personally walked through this. Although, I did not reveal all the details, there were times when God saved me from making horrible decisions that would have affected me forever. Instead, God used this situation to bring me closer to him, and now it has inspired me to write more books to help others. Could it be that the situation the devil wanted to use to keep me away from God's purpose, only pushed me right into it? Yes! Because that's how God works! He uses situations you think He can not use, and uses them to not only help you, but to help others. To God be the glory!

Self-Reflection Journal

*The **Self-Reflection Journal** is about being open and honest. It's only for you and God. Don't be ashamed. Let it all hang out. You will be better for it in the end.*

Looking back, do you feel you were ready for marriage? Why or why not?

How did you prepare for marriage?

Did you take time to observe your spouse in all seasons- angry, frustrated, sad, happy, etc.?

What red flags/concerns stood out to you concerning your spouse?

What are your values?

What are your beliefs?

Did you seek God prior to entering into marriage? If so, how did you do this?

If you could make changes within yourself, what would they be?

What characteristics did you display as a wife/husband?

What would you like yourself to display in the future?

2

Knowing Your WHY

"*Seek the Kingdom of God above all else, and live righteously, and he will give you everything you need." Matthew 6:33 NLT*

After twelve years of trying hard to make things work, my husband and I finally separated, and then divorced. It was ultimately not what I wanted. I wanted to make things work. Try counseling. Anything...but divorce. That was very hard for me, because although many times it felt like we were trying to mix oil and water together, I did love him very much and I did not want a divorce. I did not want to let go. Here a few reasons why it was such a struggle.

I always wanted to be married

The importance of marriage and family was not just portrayed by the romance industry as the ultimate goal, it is also significant in the Bible. In Genesis Chapter 2 you see that God created us to have a helpmate:

"Then the Lord God said, 'It is not good for the man to be alone. I will make a helper who is just right for him.' So the Lord God formed from the ground all the wild animals and all the birds of the sky. He brought them to the man to see what he would call them, and the man chose a name for each one. He gave names to all the livestock, all the birds of the sky, and all the wild animals. But still there was no helper just right for him. So the Lord God caused the man to fall into a deep sleep. While the man slept, the Lord God took out one of the man's ribs and closed up the opening. Then the Lord God made a woman from the rib, and he brought her to the man. 'At last!' the man exclaimed. 'This one is bone from my bone, and flesh from my flesh! She will be called 'woman,' because she was taken from 'man.' This explains why a man leaves his father and mother and is joined to his wife, and the two are united into one. Now the man and his wife were both naked, but they felt no shame." (Genesis 2:18-25 NLT)

These verses show that man and woman were made to be helpers for each other. They were made to complement each other. They were to fit together like a lock and key. Each lock has a specific key and we can not make any other key work for that lock. Even though you may get the key in the lock, it will not turn if that is not the right key for that lock.

So the desire itself to get married was natural, but the other reasons that may come along with why we want to marry may not be natural. They may be self-serving or done out of fear. We tell ourselves "they are a nice person," or "I'm not getting any younger." Sometimes it's as if we are afraid if we don't snag this person we will be alone for the rest of our life. But why do we feel we *need* to marry them? If the reasons for marriage are not solid, then the marriage is already starting off on shaky ground. The Bible tells us in Matthew 6:33 to seek Him and His kingdom first then everything we need will be given to us. Rushing into marriage without first seeking (praying to God for his advice and wisdom) really indicates we do not trust Him to bring the right person to us. The need to do it now even if it causes you to compromise on some of your beliefs, values, and goals really says you are making this decision based on fear. Fear that you are going to lose something or miss out on something. But if you lose it, was it really yours to begin with? Or if you have to change or compromise, was that person really meant for you? In my marriage I was trying to hold onto something and someone that was not mine. Legally, he was mine, yes, but he was not the man God made for me. For one, the man God made for me would not be so willing to let me go, and second we would complement each other- just like a lock fits a key. Refer back to the verses in Genesis 2:18-25 mentioned earlier. God said He did not want us to be alone. He wanted us to have a helper that was *just right* for us. And despite all of the choices we have, there is still only one person who is made just for us. Are there acceptable choices- yes. But the perfect choice is key. So from Adam, God made a woman who was just right for him, and when he saw her he recognized she was from him. Now my husband chose to marry me, but he also chose not to keep me. Had I been made for my husband, or bone of his bones and flesh of his flesh, he would not have made such an easy decision to walk away. He would have held tightly and not let go. Have you ever heard the saying, "It's cheaper to keep her?" Well, I heard it way to much. In fact, if you are hearing it in your marriage, take a step back, assess the situation, and pray. But the man, or woman, who is made for you will not use this as the means to keep you. They will keep you because they realize that you are bone of their bones and flesh of their flesh (Gen 2:23).

So why did I get married? Other than the fact that it was a deep desire of mine, I wanted to have love, legacy, and security. However, I was also afraid that I was not going to find better. I did not want to take the time to wait for the right fit, the right person.

What were some of the reasons you decided to get married? Did you not want to be alone? Did you want financial security? There are so many reasons why people decide to get married, and it is important to know what those reasons are, because when things go awry it's good to go back to the beginning. There were many times me and my ex-husband asked each other after years of marriage, "Why did we get married?" And each time we could never remember the reason why.

For every significant decision in your life, you remember why you made a particular choice. Deciding to marry someone is one of the most significant choices you will ever make, just like purchasing your first home. There are reasons why you chose that person, home, etc. So what does that tell you if you cannot remember why you married that person? Well, simply put, it's because you really don't know why you are marrying that person. You're picking that person out of fear, or you are making a decision based on your feelings without evidence of the truth that person was made for you. Now if you don't believe God has made the "just right" person for you, then this concept will be hard to understand. But if you believe that He has, then you know exactly what I am saying.

Even during writing this book I kept asking myself, "Why am I writing this book?" The difference was that I knew the answer each time. It was to help someone else who may be going through or have gone through, this difficult situation and to let them know there is hope and that God is with them. So, despite the challenges that came, as well as the many doubts, I kept coming back to my WHY. Knowing that why, and with the help of the Lord, I was able to push through the writing process. And the same will be with your marriage when you hit the hard times, the struggles, and the teary sleepless nights. Knowing *why* your marriage is important will help you get through with the help of the Lord.

I did not like to fail

I remember after getting divorced I had the overwhelming feeling of failure. I couldn't understand why I felt this way. I knew I had done everything I could to make the marriage work. I realize I was not perfect and there were many things I could have improved on, but there was no reason to feel like I had failed, especially under the cir-cumstances that ultimately led to the dissolution of the marriage. As

I mentioned earlier in this book, I like to do my best and be my best. I like the feeling of accomplishment. Even now I can see how God is changing me in that area. I no longer care about being the best, knowing it all, or even trying to be everything to everyone. I really truly just want to be the best version of myself that I can be, treat others right, and love and obey God. That is my focus.

I had conditioned myself to the point that even the marriage became something that I needed to succeed in, which was why when it didn't succeed, I felt I had failed. Not only did I feel that I failed myself, but I also felt I had failed others, even God. Everyone thought we were so happy and everything was perfect, but it wasn't. Getting a divorce was proof that things were not perfect. I could no longer hide the state of our marriage behind the big ring, nice house, and nice cars.

Also present with this earthly shame was spiritual shame. As I mentioned, I felt as if I had failed God. I knew God valued marriage. I had already messed up seeking my will over His Will by getting married in the first place, but then I couldn't even keep that going. Have you ever tried to make something work just to prove that you were not wrong in the first place? Well, this is a prime example. Not only that, I had based my perception of God's love for me by my performance. Did I check all His boxes? I felt that if I had checked off all the things God said *not* to do in the Bible then I was pleasing Him. And getting a divorce was on the list of things *not* to do. I felt I had to keep "pushing through" despite the mess.

Does this sound familiar? Have you ever felt you had to measure God's love for you by your performance? If so, I want to remind you that God loves you in spite of your mistakes. He is so in love with you that He sent His only son to die for you so you could live eternally with Him and in right relationship with Him. Here are a few scriptures to prove that:

"For this is how God loved the world: He gave his one and only Son, so that everyone who believes in him will not perish but have eternal life." (John 3:16 NLT)

"And so, dear brothers and sisters, we can boldly enter heaven's Most Holy Place because of the blood of Jesus. By his death, Jesus opened a new and life-giving way through the curtain into the Most Holy Place. And since we have a great High Priest who rules over God's house, let us go right into the presence of God with sincere hearts fully trusting him. For our guilty consciences have been sprinkled with Christ's blood to make us clean, and our bodies have been washed with pure water. Let us hold tightly without wavering to the hope we affirm, for God can be trusted to keep his promise." (Hebrews 10:19-23 NLT)

"Salvation is not a reward for the good things we have done, so none of us can boast about it. God saved you by his grace when you believed. And you can't take credit for this; it is a gift from God. For we are God's masterpiece. He has created us anew in Christ Jesus, so we can do the good things he planned for us long ago." (Ephesians 2:8-10 NLT)

These verses are only a few of the many that let us know that through Jesus Christ we have been made right with God, and it is nothing that we have earned, but have been given. Once we realize this, it opens a door of freedom and allows us to see that God looks at us through a lens of love, not a lens of judgement. The religious community have placed conditions on God's love. Meaning that we have to meet a certain standard for God to love us, or for us the be accepted by God. Unfortunately, I grew up under those religious beliefs. But as I grew under leadership that focused on the love of God rather than rules and regulations made by man, I came to understand Gods love more fully. Surprisingly, this was during the time after I had divorced where God led me to leaders in the church who were able to teach me about His love. Coincidence? Absolutely not!

Look at the Israelites. They did nothing to earn God's love and favor. Despite their mistakes God continued to bless them, not because they were good, but because of a promise God made to their ancestors. See Deuteronomy 9:3-6. In fact, if you really want to learn more about God's love for imperfect people. I encourage you to take a stroll through the Old Testament. Yes, I said the Old Testament! It has been by studying these books that I have learned more about God's character. Should you decide to do this, you will be amazed at what God will teach you!

And let me say this- there is no sin that Jesus's blood can not cleanse. He is the ultimate atonement for our sins. Therefore, even if we have missed the mark, which we will because we are not perfect, we can still have the confident assurance that he loves us and can cleanse from all sin.

Fear of the unknown

I had fear of what the future looked like alone. Twelve years of building your life with another person was a long time. Now I had to shift and determine what things looked like with just me. At times I felt that if I were a man things would have been easier. People would take me more seriously, things would go smoother, and I would be respected more. Being a single woman, I feared safety, being taken advantage of, and now the entire weight of managing a household alone. It was a lot to wrap my mind around.

I had no choice but to trust God, because it is the times when we are pushed face first into a situation that we have to learn how to sink or swim. Life did not end because I got divorced, so I had no choice but to swim. 2 Corinthians 12:9 says, "Each time he said, 'My grace is all you need. My power works best in weakness.' So now I am glad to boast about my weaknesses, so that the power of Christ can work through me."

I believe God wanted to teach me how to trust in Him. I had put my trust in my ex-husband as the provider. God wanted to show me that He was the Ultimate Provider. So I had to make choices that best suited me and my financial situation by adjusting the way I lived to accommodate one person instead of two. I didn't like it, but in order for me to swim, I had to shed the extra weight. To start, I downsized my home and car in order to have more manageable payments. Then I looked at my other monthly bills to see what could be adjusted. When I made the adjustment, little by little fear started to dissipate.

After adjusting my expenses, I decided to get anchored in a church that would allow me to grow in my knowledge and relationship with the Lord. This step was vital in moving forward. I had to learn more about God's love for me and how he wanted to take care of me in order to combat fear. 1 John 4:18 says, "Such love has no fear, because perfect love expels all fear. If we are afraid, it is for fear of punishment, and this shows that we have not fully experienced his perfect love." So if you believe God loves you, you will believe He will take care of you too. You will not believe He is punishing you by making you suffer, because God does not operate this way, the enemy does. The enemy wants you to fear God and live under a spirit of fear and punishment. God wants you to believe that you have been cleansed by the blood of Christ and confidently move forward. By deciding to believe God loves you and wants you to move forward will help you overcome those fears.

Self-Reflection Journal

What were the reasons you got married?

Have you had feelings of failure as it relates to separation/divorce? If so, what reasons do you feel contributed to this?

Do you feel God still loves you?

In what areas do you feel you were wrong? And what can you do to improve in these areas?

What steps are you taking to improve these areas?

3

Starting The Healing Process

"**D**ear *brothers and sisters, when troubles of any kind come your way, consider it an opportunity for great joy. For you know that when your faith is tested, your endurance has a chance to grow. So let it grow, for when your endurance is fully developed, you will be perfect and complete, needing nothing." James 1:2-4*

The healing process is different for everyone. This chapter focuses on the strategies that helped me heal and move forward.

Christian Counseling

If you have ever been deeply hurt, you know the healing process takes endurance. Healing doesn't happen overnight, even though the heartbreak may have. It takes time to process what happened and establish the footing to move forward. After my divorce, I began to grieve for my marriage. My Christian counselor who assisted me through this process told me that going through a divorce was often like grieving a death, except worse. This was because when a person dies you don't have to see them anymore, but with a divorce you may still have to come into contact with this person which may cause you to continue to experience the feelings of hurt. The grief process is divided into 5 stages: Denial, Anger, Bargaining, Depression, and Acceptance[2].

You may experience all of these stages, or only some. In my experience I began to experience these stages like a flood. I was in denial about my divorce. I was angry at how things ended. I began bargaining with God. I knew that even though things did not go well in the marriage, and it wasn't a good situation for me emotionally, it was still hard to let go. The depression I was already beginning to experience before the marriage ended only became worse afterwards.

After a long road of cycling through the other stages of grief multiple times, finally came acceptance. I knew I had reached a level of healing once I could talk about what happened without the conversation turning left and getting raw. I cried and prayed, which seemed non-stop. I had no idea how I even functioned during the day. All I could remember was just dreading getting out of bed and going to work with the highlight of my day being when I could get back home, crawl into bed, and cry some more. It was the worst heartbreak I had felt in my whole life. Honestly, I can't even put into words how hard emotionally this time was for me. Again, there are so many things I can't share. I was so broken. Just so very very broken.

I remember going to a well-known divorce ministry. It had great reviews and many positive testimonies from people who had gone through the program. I went to three meetings, and each time, I felt horrible afterwards. Whatever steps I had made forward, I took three steps back after leaving the meeting. It always took me back to the beginning stages of my hurt and anger. I believe it was because my heart broke for what the other people were going through. So not only was I hurting for them, I was hurting for myself. It was more than I could bear emotionally. How in the world did Jesus bear all of our burdens on the cross?

When I saw what these meetings were taking me through emotionally, I decided not to go back, even though they were nationally known and acclaimed. Instead, I searched for a Christian counselor who counseled me individually, and when the time was right, I joined a divorce group with two other women led by my counselor. We were all being counseled by her individually and then would meet with our group at certain times.

I felt getting a Christian counselor was the first step in my healing process. At least, I was not too prideful to know I needed professional help. And there is nothing wrong with seeking the assistance of a professional. Sadly, some of the religious community will condemn you for seeking counseling, making you feel as if your faith is not strong enough to see you through. This too, is another lie on what God expects from you. The truth is God does not expect you to do anything alone. He values community and relationships. He will also use anyone He chooses to assist you. The religious community puts stipulations on who can assist you. As Christians, we have to stop putting God in a box and allow Him to work as He chooses. I digress......

I knew I could not make it through this time alone. Speaking with a Christian counselor helped me gain a realistic perspective on the situation. Through sound biblical insight and practical truths, I began to see my unhealthy thought processes. I began to rebuild my relationship with God. It wasn't that I had walked away from Him, but I needed Him to rebuild me from the inside out-make right what was wrong and move on from the old.

Isaiah 43:18 says, "But forget all that- it is nothing compared to what I am going to do. For I am about to do something new. See, I have already begun! Do you not see it? I will make a pathway through the wilderness. I will create rivers in the dry wasteland." I was trying desperately to hold on to something that had ended. God said don't hold on to the old, move on to the new things He has in store. I had to take a step forward if I was going to make it.

The important thing to remember is to find what works best for you. Everyone will have a suggestion- listen to it, and determine if that is something that would work for you. If not, thank them and continue to move forward until you find what works.

Do the thoughts of being alone scare you? Being alone was very scary for me. I feared there would be no one to help if things got rough and stressful. But every time I looked back over the past years of singleness, after my divorce, I only see God's hand of provision. Not once did I not have everything I needed, but he even supplied me with things I wanted. It's like He was showing me that He was my source-not anyone else. I had come to a place where I had in many ways exalted my ex-husband over God, because he was such a good provider. I had forgotten who allowed him to provide. I forgot the Lord was the ultimate provider- Jehovah Jireh. Thank God I know now! The devil thought if he took away who I thought was my provider, then I would crumble. But God! God showed me that I was strong in Him, not on my own. Not only did He meet me financially, He met me spiritually and emotionally. I began to thrive. My depression had eased. I found happiness and peace that I never remembered experiencing before. After selling our old home and moving into a home of my own (which was a whole different stress LOL), I remember coming home from work one day and laying on the couch. The peacefulness that surrounded me was so loud that it got my attention. I remember thinking, "Wow. I never knew how much peace I was missing until now." I thanked God then, and every day afterward for giving me peace.

Personal Support

Another thing that was helpful, in addition to the Christian counselor, was my close circle of family and friends. I talked to my mother almost everyday. She was so helpful with words of wisdom, because she too had experienced the very same thing. Listening to her words of advice was invaluable. Not only were her words helpful during the divorce, but afterwards as I began to experience other challenges associated with mending the heart. I also had a very close friend named Kimberly. I was able to be honest with her about how I was feeling and she would give me sound Christian advice. Most of all, I knew my mother and Kimberly were praying for me. You don't need a large circle, and you don't need to broadcast everything that's going on to everyone. All you need is a small circle of people you can trust, who can lift you up in prayer, and who you can confide in when times get tough.

Cutting Ties

Cutting ties with things, and sometimes people, are necessary to heal. I had to find a new way to work. It took me a little longer to get there, but I didn't have to drive by my ex's house every morning and every night. We didn't have the same friends so that was very helpful. But I found that when I purchased my new home, going to another city where everything was new was even more helpful. It was like a fresh start. Now I realize that is not feasible for everyone, but I tried staying in the same house, driving the same car, living in the same town, and that did not work for me. I had to cut ties and start fresh. But if you can not do this, then ask God what it is that you need to do for you. Again, it's not about my recommendations, it's about what is going to work best for you. One more thing....that "let's stay friends" option isn't a good idea either....now let's move on.

Get Connected

Getting connected to a community church group or finding other leisure activities to get your mind off the situation is helpful also. You have to build relationships in order to continue to thrive. I was attending a wonderful church at the time of the divorce, but I was led to attend different churches until the Lord led me to the right one. Each and every church was essential for each stage in my journey. Ecclesiastes 3:1-8 tells us there is a season for everything. So, what may have worked for you in the past may not always work for you in the future. It's a process of change. We have to be open to the Lord's leading. If not, we can get stagnant and left behind.

Journaling

Journaling is a helpful way to get out emotions that may be inappropriate to say to the other person. I'm just saying! Journaling really helped me release some hurt and anger. I remember coming across the journal last year as I was cleaning out my home. When I opened it up and read some of the pages, I reflected on where God has bought me from, thanked Him, and then threw it away. When my season of needing that journal left, so did the journal. You can't afford to keep those toxic thoughts around, because the devil will use your mind as a breeding ground. Philippians 4:8 says, "And no, dear brothers and sisters, one final thing. Fix your thoughts on what is true, and honorable, and right, and pure, and lovely, and admirable. Think about things that are excellent and worthy of praise." Now you may be thinking, "Well some of the things I am thinking about are true!" While that may be true, are those "true" thoughts only reminding you of how you were wronged? If so, you have to shift those thoughts to things that are praiseworthy. For example, when I started remembering all the bad things, because of course they come to mind, I remember saying "Thank you God for your peace and provision." You just can't dwell on the bad. What you continue to think on is what will stay prevalent in your mind, which will ultimately affect your attitude. Proverbs 23:7 NKJV says, "for as a man thinks in his heart, so is he."

Protect Your Heart

I also need to mention that you are very vulnerable during this time. It will be easy to set your sites on other people looking for the love and affection that you may feel you did not receive from your spouse, or as something to just take away the hurt. But I caution you on focusing your sites on other people during this time. Allow yourself time to heal. Take some time to focus on God without interference. I found myself in the same situation only to go through heartbreak and rejection a second time. Not everyone who shows interest is truly interested. Some are there for selfish motives and you must be careful of that.

So how long does the healing process last? Well, that's different for everyone. It has been six years since my divorce, and there is still a level of healing that is taking place. But it's more of a personal refinement, not the grief process. The divorce and what happened no longer bothers me. I am allowing God to make me into a new person, because I do not want to carry what were problems in my past marriage into my next marriage, nor do I want to be the same person I was then. I want to be better. I am continuing to build my firm foundation on Christ by deepening my relationship with Him, so when my next relationship comes, The Rock (which is Jesus), will not be moved. My next relationship should only enhance my current relationship with Christ, and if I see that it's taking away from it, then I know that relationship is not for me, or from God. Christ must stay first. I will no longer put Christ on the backburner. It's a non-negotiable for me.

Self-Reflection Journal

Did you experience the stages of the grief process? If so, how did you handle them?

What avenues did you use for healing- group support, counseling, etc.?

If you haven't sought counseling, why is that?

What fears do you have about being alone, or moving forward?

Who is your support circle? How have they helped you?

What are you using to help channel your emotions in a healthy way?

4

Overcoming Rejection

"*You made all the delicate, inner parts of my body and knit me together in my mother's womb. Thank you for making me so wonderfully complex! Your workmanship is marvelous—how well I know it." Psalms 139:13-14*

"*How precious are your thoughts about me, O God. They cannot be numbered! I can't even count them; they outnumber the grains of sand! And when I wake up, you are still with me!" Psalms 139:17-18*

I wanted to start this chapter off with these verses, because when you start to feel rejected it is often because you have allowed someone else's perspective of us to shape who you are. You must first know God's love for you, and then you must know and love who you are as a person.

Ask yourself these questions:

- Who are you?
- What makes you special?
- Who made you?
- Who loves you?

Remember Who You Are

Other people and past mistakes do not define you. God defines who you are, and you define who you are based upon your understanding of who you are in Christ. I want you to think about the previous questions. Knowing the answer to these questions is very important. You need to know yourself, because if you don't define who you are someone else will. I initially wanted to start this chapter off with the different reasons why I felt rejected, but honestly that doesn't even matter. The main reason I felt rejected was because I let someone else, and the situation, define me. I had to remember *who* I was and *whose* I was. I had to remember my value and worth. We all make mistakes, but I also feel many of us strive to do the best we can too. There are times we have to give ourselves grace. Don't worry about what other people may think of you because of your divorce or your past mistakes. No one knows your situation. They may think they know, but they do not.

Take a moment to think about how you are feeling. Do you feel loved by yourself and others? Who are those who love you? Remembering everyone who loves you can help lift your spirits when you start to feel down or unloved. Even if it's one or two people- you are still loved!! It is a tactic of the devil to lie to you, make you feel inadequate, and steal your joy. But God says in John 10:10, "The thief's purpose is to steal and kill and destroy. My purpose is to give them a rich and satisfying life." That means God wants us to be happy. He does not want you feeling down, depressed, and rejected. So, remind yourself that you are loved. And if you can't think of anyone who loves you, remember that God loves you.

"For this is how God loved the world: He gave his one and only Son, so that everyone who believes in him will not perish but have eternal life." (John 3:17)

Give Yourself Grace

You must remember we all make mistakes. Whether those mistakes were intentional or unintentional doesn't really matter at this time. What does matter is what we learned from those mistakes, and what changes we can make in the future to prevent those mistakes from happening again. Your past mistakes don't define you unless you allow them too. Do not dwell on your mistakes. Acknowledge them as areas needing improvement and seek God's help in making the change. Isaiah 43:25 says, "I-yes, I alone-will blot out your sins for my own sake and will never think of them again." God forgives our sins so He doesn't have to think about them again; therefore, do not continue to dwell on your past mistakes. If God doesn't want to remember them, then neither should you.

I feel I need to say this. I am not making light of the situation of divorce. I firmly believe in the covenant of marriage. But there are some situations and circumstances that are out of our control, or sometimes it's a consequence of our actions. Whether it's a result of our behaviors, or someone else's, the truth is there is usually fault that lies with both sides. We should take time to seek God in prayer and ask him to show us what we did wrong, and what areas need to be changed. It's easy to ask a friend after telling them your side of the story, but even if they were the type of friend who would tell you the truth no matter what, they still were not in the situation with you. Proverbs 21:2 says, "People may be right in their own eyes, but the Lord examines their heart." God is the only one who can truly show you what is wrong. I remember thinking I was the victim, along with the long list of things he did wrong, but God had to show me where I had blame also. However, once He shows you take note and move forward. Do not continue to dwell on it.

Move Forward

You cannot continue to dwell on the past. Mistakes will come, but you have to get back up and keep moving. Proverbs 24:16 is a perfect example of moving forward. It says, "The godly may trip seven times, but they will get up again." Psalms 37:24 says, "Though they stumble, they will never fall, for the Lord holds them by the hand." So, God understands we will make mistakes, but He says that you will not fall for He will hold you by the hand!

Taking these steps are important in moving forward:

- Acknowledge the situation in front of you and the truth of why things happened the way they did.
- Acknowledge the true feelings you are experiencing (hurt, pain, anger, unforgiveness, rejection, etc.) and give them to God. Ask Him to help you get rid of all things that are not right in his eyes.

Some of my favorite scriptures to pray are:

Psalms 139: 23-24 NLT, "Search me, Oh God, and know my heart; test me and know my anxious thoughts. Point out anything in me that offends you, and lead me along the path of everlasting life." I like this verse because it allows me to present myself to God for examination and ask, "What is it in me that may be causing me to feel rejected?" Are you fearful? Do you lack confidence? Do you care more about what someone else says about you than what God says about you? By taking the time to present the feeling of rejection to God will allow Him to give you insight on what needs to be changed.

Psalms 51:10 KJV, "Create in me a clean heart, O God; And renew a right spirit within me." This scripture says, "Make me a better person Lord!" Now you may be thinking, "Why do I need to be a better person? I wasn't the one who did something wrong." But allowing the rejection to sit in our minds and hearts too long will cause other feelings to develop, such as resentment, unforgiveness, or depression.

True change always starts on the inside before you can take physical steps in moving forward.

Psalms 56:8 NLT, "You keep track of all my sorrows. You have collected all my tears in your bottle. You have recorded each one in your book." Even though I'm giving examples of how to overcome rejection, I don't want to forget that actually feeling rejected is hurtful. Regardless of why you feel rejected, part of overcoming it is acknowledging the hurt that comes with it. As I was reading my Bible one day, I came across this scripture and I remember how comforting it was to know that God saw every one of my tears. He doesn't just brush past your feelings. He said He collected each one and recorded it in your book. Doesn't that spring forth a hope that He will make everything right?

Get your mind in order

Do not listen to the lies of the devil or continue to dwell on the negative things that happened. As we continue to think about those things, they will take root in our hearts and limit our progress forward. "For as a man thinks in his heart so is he" (Proverbs 23:7 KJV). Meaning, what you think about, you will act upon, and will shape who you are as a person.

Furthermore, the Bible says, "We use God's mighty weapons, not worldly weapons, to knock down the strongholds of human reasoning and to destroy false arguments. We destroy every proud obstacle that keeps people from knowing God. We capture their rebellious thoughts and teach them to obey Christ" (2 Corinthians 10:4-5 NLT).

Not to make this sound like a bunch of religious jargon, but our emotions and actions will follow what we focus our mind on. We must make a conscious effort to focus on the right things, and it will not just be a one-time thing. The devil constantly attacks your mind in efforts to control our actions. We must refuse to listen to his lies and focus our attention on God. Please hear me when I say- *constantly*.

It's a battle you cannot fight and win on your own. You must ask God to help you, and you must continue to read and study the word so you will know what the truth is.

Get around the right people

It may be necessary to disconnect yourself from certain people in your life, such as people who may continue to remind you of your failures, or those who do not have a positive effect on you. Believe it or not, there are actually people who do not want to see you do better. Those are the people you have to leave behind. You need people who will encourage you, lift you up, educate, and train you in new and positive things. Yes, you may hear, "Oh so you think you are better than me now?" But do not fall for that trick of manipulation. You do not owe anyone rights to your life. If you want to do better, then you need to be around people who can help you do so.

Rejection is a part of life that we will all experience at some point. My grandmother used to always say, "Just keep on living." Meaning, what you think you may never experience now, may be something you experience in the future. It's really how we choose to handle the rejection that impacts us. Rejection is only rejection if you accept the opinion that was given. If it is not your belief then it doesn't alter your perception of yourself. For example, I used to think I was overweight, and in actuality I was. No one actually told me I was overweight. But it was my own perception that inspired me to lose weight. I didn't like how I felt, so I made a change. Now if I liked my previous weight and it didn't bother me, then it would not bother me to hear someone say I was overweight. I would say, "Oh, well!" But it's when I agree with them that puts me on their same belief level.

So, take your own self-inventory. Think about what you like about yourself, and what would you like to change, etc. But make sure the changes you want to make are because you want them changed, not because you want others' approval.

Self-Reflection Journal

What five words describe you and why?

What makes you special?

What would you like to change to make yourself better?

List the names of those who love you.

What do you love most about yourself?

What steps are you taking to bring positive changes to your life?

5

You Are Not Being Punished

"*And I am convinced that nothing can ever separate us from God's love. Neither death nor life, neither angels nor demons, neither our fears for today nor our worries about tomorrow—not even the powers of hell can separate us from God's love. No power in the sky above or in the earth below—indeed, nothing in all creation will ever be able to separate us from the love of God that is revealed in Christ Jesus our Lord.*" Romans 8:38-39

How many of you have felt that God's love is determined by your level of worship, prayer, Sunday attendance, or the number of good things you have done? And have you ever felt that if something bad happens to you it's because you have obviously done something wrong? I have to admit that I have felt like that frequently. I'm still working on learning that God loves me not because of my performance, but because He's a loving God. We talked about this in the last chapter.

Sometimes we feel that when we go through hard times, we are being punished for something we did wrong. That is not always the case. I do believe that we experience things in life as a result of how we have lived. The Bible terms this as sowing and reaping, and others call it Karma. However, there are times when there is nothing we have done to cause bad things to happen, they just do. I can honestly say that I did not feel my divorce happened, because I thought I was being punished. That's probably the one feeling I did not have! I knew what kind of a person I was, and I knew I did everything I could to make it work. What happened to cause my divorce were seeds that I have never sown in life, and I believe there was absolutely nothing I could have done to avoid it. However, I do believe that although I didn't reap the good seeds I sowed in that relationship they certainly will be reaped in the next one.

People make their own decisions, and you cannot blame yourself or hold yourself responsible for another person's decisions. I simply wanted to address this issue if it was something you were experiencing. This is where having a solid counselor is beneficial. They can help you identify wrong or unhealthy patterns of thinking. When I got divorced, I never felt I was being punished, but I did have a "guilt" mentality. I had been conditioned to believe everything that was going wrong in the marriage was my fault, and I was constantly apologizing in order to create peace. I did not even realize I had established this mentality until it was pointed out to me by my counselor, and what a difference it made in my healing process! Without her assistance I would have been burdened down with unnecessary blame. Take time to assess your thought patterns. Are there any unhealthy patterns that need to be addressed? If so, take time to write them down in the *Self-Reflection Journal* at the end of the chapter. And remember that even though unfortunate things happen, there is still room to turn a bad situation into a better one. God made us a promise in Romans 8:28, "And we know that God causes everything to work together for the good of those who love God and are called according to his purpose for them." Let's focus our attention to the words *His Purpose* and *God's Love.*

His Purpose

When we step out of the will of God anything can happen. As I mentioned earlier in this book, I did not take the time to seek God's will before getting married. I made decisions based on my own wants and desires. So, when you make decisions based on what you want, then God is not required to bless it. But, when we follow His leading and instructions, He will honor His word and bless it. See Deuteronomy 28:1-14, which outlines the blessings God will give us for following Him, and the results of not following.

Stepping outside of God's Will opens the door for difficulty. It says, "God, I got this. I don't need your help." A good example of this is in Genesis Chapter 16, which talks about how Sarai (also known as Sara) went outside of God's will and used her servant Hagar to have a child instead of waiting on God. After that happened, she was not pleased with the turn of events that transpired, and then had the nerve to blame Abram for her mistake! God had made Abram (also known as Abraham) a promise in Genesis 15:4-5 that he would give him a son and that his descendants would be as numerous as the stars in the sky.

Another example of the consequences of stepping outside of God's will is in 2 Samuel Chapters 11 through 12:1-23. It refers to how David went outside of the will of God and slept with Bathsheba, and when he found out she was pregnant conspired to kill her husband, Uriah, in order to marry her. The child that was conceived from this act ended up dying.

I know these are Old Testament stories, and sometimes those stories seem extreme in consequences at times, but we must not overlook the big picture- the consequences of stepping out of alignment with God lead to unwanted events. Divorce could be a result of those consequences, but if we get back into alignment with God there is still hope. He says in Jeremiah 29:11, "For I know the plans I have for you," says the Lord. "They are plans for good and not for disaster, to give you a future and a hope." Now is divorce destined for those marriages that started outside the will of God? No, not necessarily. God can bring all things into alignment if both parties are willing. Both parties have to be willing, not just one. If either person does not want to continue in the marriage we cannot make them, because God gives us all free will and He will not override that.

God's Love

God loves you and wants the best for you. We just read that in Jeremiah 29:11, and Romans 8:38-39. God only wants us to stay in alignment with His will not to control us, but to protect us. There is protection when we are in alignment with God (see Psalms 91). The protection is not only physical, but it also includes protection from unnecessary heartbreaks and circumstances. Key word to remember- unnecessary! Keep in mind that even though we may be in line with God does not mean we will not experience difficult times.

"What shall we say about such wonderful things as these? If God is for us, who can ever be against us? Since he did not spare even his own Son but gave him up for us all, won't he also give us everything else? Who dares accuse us whom God has chosen for his own? No one—for God himself has given us right standing with himself. Who then will condemn us? No one—for Christ Jesus died for us and was raised to life for us, and he is sitting in the place of honor at God's right hand, pleading for us. Can anything ever separate us from Christ's love? Does it mean he no longer loves us if we have trouble or calamity, or are persecuted, or hungry, or destitute, or in danger, or threatened with death? (As the Scriptures say, "For your sake we are killed every day; we are being slaughtered like sheep.") No, despite all these things, overwhelming victory is ours through Christ, who loved us." (Romans 8:31-37 NLT).

This passage does a great job explaining this, especially (verses 35-37) which tells us that it doesn't mean God does not love us if we experience trouble, but overwhelming victory is ours *because* He loves us.

Now remember the title of this book, "Divorced But Not Defeated." It is not titled, "What Does God Say About Divorce?" So I do not feel it is in the authority God has given me to tell you if divorce is right or wrong, but what He did tell me to do was tell of His goodness and love despite divorce. If you want a biblical view of divorce and whether it is right or wrong, go to the Word of God and read it for yourself, for there are many scriptures related to divorce; but also seek your pastor or other Christian leader whose advice you trust to gain more understanding of these scriptures. I have to stick with what the Lord has called me to do, so I am going to stay in the lane God has given me.

Lastly, I want to say that divorce was the most difficult, heart-wrenching thing that I had ever experienced, and frankly never want to experience again. But out of that heartbreak, God has proved faithful to me and has shown me each and every day that He loves me, He is with me, and He is continuing to bless me. He used this heartbreak to bring me closer to Him and restore our relationship. He also used it to show me that He is the one who provides for me, not another person (or even myself). Furthermore, He used this situation to show me that my value and worth and is not defined by another person, only by Him. He has shown me that His love is unfailing towards me, and that He has wonderful plans for my future. I believe the same goes for you. It does not matter if you are divorced because of something you have done, or someone else, God has good in store for you...believe that! Submit the situation, and yourself, to God and He will show you all the good things He has in store. Remember there will be people who will want to remind you of what you have done, or even make you feel "less of" because you have experienced divorce, but remember WHO you are and WHOSE you are!

<u>Self-Reflection Journal</u>

Do you feel your divorce is part of punishment from God? If so, why?

Have you identified any unhealthy thinking patterns you need to change?

Think about ways God has shown His love for you and list them here.

6

Restoration Time

"*But forget all that—it is nothing compared to what I am going to do. For I am about to do something new. See, I have already begun! Do you not see it? I will make a pathway through the wilderness. I will create rivers in the dry wasteland.*" Isaiah 43:18-19

Have you ever lost something and thought, "One day I will get that back. I will have that again." Maybe the loss was money, possessions, a job, or something else significant in your life. Maybe in your divorce you lost love, time, a family, a home, a job, a church, or a geographical location? All the things you loved with hopes of one day getting it back?

Well, I believe God will restore to you what you lost and make it even better than it was before.

I remember being so upset that I had to sell my home, change churches (more than once), change some medical professionals, and give up my car and truck all as a trickle effect from the divorce. The pill is easier to swallow when you voluntarily give up certain things, but it hits differently when the choice is involuntary. But the thing that really rattled my cage and made me the most upset, was the time that was lost. If you really want to upset me, waste my time or waste my money! Hey, I'm still a work in progress! Twelve years, prime years I might add, were lost because of someone else's decisions. It was very discouraging and at times made me very angry, if I'm being honest.

Again, I accepted the fact that I entered a marriage that I believe was not God's Will for me, but there was also a lot of time devoted, and other things I could not get back. Then God began to place hope within my heart. A hope that things would get better and I would one day get back what I lost. What I wanted stretched far beyond material things. I wanted a husband that truly loved and appreciated me. I wanted a chance to have a family. Just to know I was truly loved and irreplaceable- that's what I wanted. I needed God to restore the time so I could have a chance to experience that. That was the *better* I was looking for.

I began to hear teachings on restoration. Now restoration as it relates to Christian teaching was not something I was familiar with. I had heard different sermons related to restoration, but it wasn't until I started listening to the teachings of Apostle Joshua Giles, of Joshua Giles Ministries[3], that really helped me understand restoration. He taught on restoration as God not only restoring what you lost, but also stated when God restores you, He will restore you to an even better place than you were before. Did you hear me, an even *better* place. That really blew my mind and stuck out to me. I remember saying, "God will restore me to better?" Wow, only God can do that! God is so gracious that He says, not only will He give you back what was taken from you, but He will make you better than before.

Now as I said before, God had already started to put hope within my heart- hope that things would get better, but this word from Apostle Giles came six years after my divorce and even more hope began to grow. A type of hope that fueled me during tough days, and times. Days where I felt no one loved or appreciated me. Days where I was tired of doing life alone and without the covering God intended for me to have as a woman. Days where I asked, "God do you even see me...your daughter?" Then one day God led me to a scripture, "You keep track of all my sorrows. You have collected all my tears in your bottle" (Psalms 56:8). God saw me and took account of every tear and every sorrow I was experiencing. He did not say, "You handle this on your own," nor did He ever make me feel that since I was divorced that He didn't care about my happiness. I truly believe that as God was healing me on the inside, He was also simultaneously preparing me for greater. There are so many scriptures that relate to this, including the focus scripture at the beginning of the chapter, but I will note a couple more below:

Psalms 37:23, "The Lord directs the steps of the godly. He delights in every detail of their lives."

Psalms 71:21, "You will restore me to even greater honor and comfort me once again."

There is another marriage in the future for me, and it will be better than I imagined, because I have invited God into the decision process. I have asked Him to direct my relationships, and to bring the spouse he has for me...my covenant partner. Although I made mistakes in the past, He is making sure that my future will be brighter, because it will be well-established in Him.

Take a moment to think about what you have lost, and what you want to experience in your future. Write them down in the **_Self-Reflection Journal_** at the end of the chapter. God wants to hear from you!

In the waiting

So, if it was six years afterwards when I felt this hope, what did I do in years one through five? Well as I mentioned in the previous chapters, I was going through the healing process, self-reflecting, letting go of anger, pride and unforgiveness, as well as, redeveloping my relationship with God. That process doesn't happen in two weeks. It's a progression and a refinement. Once you make it to a certain level, there may be times when you realize you need to go back to a previous level because you didn't learn everything you needed to learn. How did I know this? Well, when certain tests came my way I failed miserably! So, I had to start again. How many of you hate starting over? I know I do. But it was necessary. I knew I had to be better.…. I *needed* to be better. But it was this word in restoration that gave me the push to continue and develop a hope that God had better in store for me.

So now I'm in the season of *The Waiting*. The season of waiting is when you lean into God, pray for His direction, and wait for Him to answer. It's very important to wait on God and not get ahead of Him. See that was my problem before, I didn't know how to wait. I moved ahead of God and ended up in failure. Psalm 37:7 says, "Be still in the presence of the Lord, and wait patiently for him to act." I feel the waiting is the hardest part, because I like things instantly. I don't like surprises… I like to know now! God is going to move in His timing, because His timing is always perfect. However, waiting doesn't mean you are sitting and doing nothing. No, you actually have to be active during this time. Active in seeking God, active in growing your faith, active in learning how to hear God's voice. Active in getting healthier, getting rid of bad habits, and paying down debts so you don't enter into another relationship with these types of old burdens. No, you can't just sit around and do nothing. Remember, if God is going to restore what you lost and make it even better than before, then He has to make *YOU* better than before. As the Bible says, you can't put old wine in new wineskins because they will not hold the new wine. And we also don't put a new patch on an old garment, because it won't match.

Luke 5:36-38 NIV says, "He told them this parable: No one tears a piece out of a new garment to patch an old one. Otherwise, they will have torn the new garment, and the patch from the new will not match the old. And no one pours new wine into old wineskins. Otherwise, the new wine will burst the skins; the wine will run out and the wineskins will be ruined. No, new wine must be poured into new wineskins."

How can I expect God to bring me better if I don't allow Him to make me better first? If I don't become better, then I will mess up the better he has in store for me. I won't be ready to accept it, I won't know how to treat it, and I won't know how to take care of it. God is teaching me how to take care of His best. But to do this we have to go through a waiting period. A time of refinement to take out the old. This is not an easy period. When God changes us, it is not comfortable. It is hard and unpleasant, sometimes to the point where you may want to say forget it.

Luke 5:39 says, "And no one after drinking old wine wants the new, for they say, 'The old is better.'"

Why is that? Why do people crave and settle for the old instead of the new? Those who drink wine know that the older the wine the better it tastes, but I believe this scripture deals with settling. Settling for the old, because we don't want the work of establishing the new. Building something that is new takes time and effort. So in order for us to become someone better, or someone new, we are going to have to put in work. And this is the time when you decide if you are willing to settle for the old, or if you are going to establish the new.

An example of settling for the old would be saying, "Well they are just going to have to love me the way I am. I'm not changing for anyone." And that is true to a point, but it is also a way to skip the refining process that makes you a better person. You may also tell yourself that God loves you the way you are, which is also true, but can also be an excuse resist change. Can you see how certain thoughts in your mind can stop change? Are you willing to give up the old and press forward toward the new? Remember it's the end product that makes it all worth it.

Here are a few steps to help you with the waiting process. All the steps that I am going through myself:

Guard your eyes and ears. You may hear preachers say "guard your eye gates and ear gates." That isn't just a religious saying that sounds good, there is much truth in it. I noticed that when I watched anything I wanted and listened to anything I wanted it made it harder to stay in line with God. It made it harder to focus on God. The things we watch and listen to resonate in our minds and those things we think about make a way into our hearts. Then we start to believe those things as truth, and our actions start to follow. The devil will use anything to get you off track, and it starts with songs and TV shows that seem harmless. All he needs is a small opportunity to get his foot in the door. For example, there was a particular artist I LOVED to listen to. I was a HUGE fan. I listened to her songs often not thinking anything of it, because I felt it was just a song. But as God started to change certain things about me, I noticed that when I began to listen to her music those things I had put in my past began to rise back up. The ungodly desires I had let go of began to come back, which actually started in my dreams. The first time that happened, I thought it was just a coincidence. Then it happened a second and third time. It was then I realized, through the help of the Holy Spirit, that it only happened after I listened to her music. So even though I didn't want to give up listening to her music, I had to for the sake of refinement and a greater purpose. Thank God I did not act on any of those old desires, but had I not stopped listening to her music the devil would have continued to reintroduce those thoughts back into my mind with those dreams, and I probably would have ended up acting on it. In addition to that, God is teaching me the importance of casting out thoughts that are not of Him. Had I not learned what He was teaching me, I would not have recognized the devil's tactics.

Watch your inner circle. Everyone is not for you, and everyone does not want you to succeed. I have never been one who had many friends or hung around a lot of people. My friends were few, and my inner circle (those who knew the personal details of my life) were even fewer. I had to learn this truth the hard way a long time ago. Some people will use you to get what they want. They will smile in your face and talk behind your back. Some will even secretly hope for you to fail when they have verbalized they want you to succeed. You have to get the Lord's leading on who He wants close to you. Will He use people who are not in your inner circle to help you to succeed? He absolutely will! He will use anything and anyone to carry out His plan. But that doesn't mean you have to have them at your house every night, or invite them to personal gatherings. The people who spend personal time with me are those whose words and actions line up. Those who have shown me through their actions they want the best for me. Those with truth and integrity. I am even careful about who I ask to pray for me, because I need to know those people's words line up with God's words, and even my words. We can't be praying on two different wavelengths.

Even Jesus had a small circle. Joshua Giles in his recent book *Prophetic Reset: 40 Days to Aligning with God's Plan for Your Life*[4], did an excellent job describing Jesus and his relationships with certain groups of people. See pages 199-202. Jesus knew who he needed as part of his inner circle, to work in the ministry, and who to keep at arm's length. John 2:24-25 NLT says, "But Jesus didn't trust them, because he knew all about people. No one needed to tell him about human nature, for he knew what was in each person's heart." Now you might be saying, "Of course Jesus knew what was in their hearts, He knew everything!" Yes, that may be true, but if we ask him, he will give us the same wisdom and discernment. He may tell you a particular person is not for you, or you may see it by the actions they display.

Set time for God. Setting time for God can include a number of things such as reading the Bible, fasting, quiet time, praying, journaling, or meditation. Your private time with God will look different than someone else's. The important thing is to make it personal. When you make it personal, it allows you to go deeper with God, because now you are not just doing it to check off a checkbox on a list. It allows you to develop an intimate relationship with God that stretches outside of a specific routine. I will give you an example, again not to recommend how your time needs to be, but it may help those who do not currently have a routine. Each morning I wake up, I lay in bed a few moments while it's still quiet, and think. It is the time of day that is the most still and my mind is the most clear. I try and concentrate to see if I hear the Lord speaking about anything in particular, or see if anything comes to mind that I need to pay attention to. I also take this time to write down any dreams that I may have dreamt of the night before and ask God what the meaning is. There are times when I get clarity during that time, and if not I still make sure I write it down in case God brings an explanation at a later time. I've noticed the more time I set aside for God the more He may bring a dream to me, especially during times of fasting, or times when I ask God specifically to bring clarity on a certain subject. Once I get out of the bed and get ready for the day, I go downstairs, make a cup of coffee, and read in the Bible or follow along with a devotional for guided reading. I pray and then set forth to my day. On my drive to work, I do not play any music. I make this my quiet time, because it is during this time that God often speaks to me, and gives me direction on different things I have been praying about. I feel it is because my mind is still geared towards Him from the meditation when I woke up, and the reading of His Word is still fresh in my spirit. I also have not had time to get upset by different things of the day at this time! When I leave work, depending on my mood, I will either pray, listen to worship music, or a Christian audiobook. Something to keep me encouraged. Once I get home, I usually relax by performing activities I like. When I go to bed I lay and reflect on the day, and pray again about different issues I'm concerned about (casting my cares on God), pray for others, etc. This routine may vary based on the day, but the important thing is I let the Spirit lead me, and I make sure I have "quiet time" during the day. It's the time when my spirit is telling the Holy Spirit "Speak Lord." We can not hear from God if there is constant noise in the background.

Ok, now you may be thinking, "What does this have to do with re-covering from a divorce?" It's about shifting your mind and emotions to God. It helps with keeping you from being depressed when looking at your situation, or remembering the past hurts. Past hurts cut deep, some deeper than others, but you can't dwell there. We have to set our mind on God and other things. Again, this is my routine. Take time to figure out what works for you.

Fast. Fasting helps gain clarity and direction, because it causes you to focus more time on God. It's intentional timing. It helps to clear distractions by taking some things off of our "To Do" list. I won't go too much into types of fasting, I just want to highlight that it has been a great way to get closer to God and gain more clarity and understand-ing. But there are many resources available if you want to learn more, for example Stephanie Ike has some great videos on You Tube con-cerning fasting.

Pray. Praying doesn't have to be long and drawn out prayers of many words. It can be simple. "Lord help me." "Lord, I need you." "Lord, I don't know which way to go." Or it could be, "Lord I'm still so very hurt and upset by this divorce. Please help me heal past this hurt."

It's ok to acknowledge exactly how you feel in prayer. Because I'm going to tell you, my prayers were not this simple or light. Can I just be real? This book is meant to be a help, but there were some real feel-ings that I needed help with. Again, hurt can cut deep, especially when words were said that made you wonder how someone who suppos-edly loved you could say. Times of asking God why He isn't doing any-thing about the situation, and so on. You can be real with God. Tell Him exactly how you feel, because He already knows anyway. God is not a spiritual being that just sits high in the clouds on his throne and judges you. He truly cares about you and how you are feeling. I also know that He is working things out for you, it's just that you may not see it at that time.

Watch what you say. I'm learning more and more how our words can affect our lives. Words are powerful because they move the spiritual realm. Proverbs 18:21 says, "The tongue can bring death or life; those who love to talk will reap the consequences." Try to use your words to help build you up during this time. For example, instead of saying "No one loves me or will ever love me." Try saying, "I'm grateful that God loves me, and He will send the right person my way who will love me too." Positive affirmations will build your life in a positive direction instead of using negative words or words of defeat to keep you stuck in the same place. Remember this chapter deals with restoration- restoring your life. We can't pray to God and ask Him to restore us and then use our words to tear down what He is trying to build. We have to continue to speak in alignment with what we are praying.

Stay encouraged- Listening to sermons, communicating with fellow believers, reading the Bible, participating in hobbies you enjoy, etc., are all great ways to stay encouraged. Staying encouraged is a constant assignment. Everyday I have to stay encouraged just dealing with everyday life, because of course everything doesn't center around experiencing divorce. Life itself needs encouragement! It is also helpful to write down any dreams and visions, or future goals you have for when times get difficult or in times of doubt. Go back and remind yourself of where you are going. Keep speaking the Word of God and believing until it comes to pass, or God brings you something better.

Avoid unnecessary detours. I mentioned this earlier in the book, don't get swept away by the "next" relationship too soon. Take time to get to know yourself, and determine your goals and direction before entertaining other romantic relationships. The healing process is very important, because it puts you as the priority. If you don't take time to focus on you and what you need/want, someone else will determine that for you. Also, experiencing another heartbreak or emotional letdown too soon may cause the old wounds to resurface, and sometimes that stings just a little more than the original wounds. Be careful of people who are out to waste your time. Stay focused.

I pray that after reading this chapter, you have a better understanding of God's love for you. Take a moment to reflect on some of the topics discussed and write them down in the ***Self-Reflection Journal***.

Self-Reflection Journal

What have you lost that you would like God to restore?

What areas do you need God's help in improving? For example, healthy physical and financial habits, reestablishing your relationship with God, etc.

Can God trust you with His best? If not, why? Use this as a way to pray to God and ask for His assistance in making you a better person in order to prepare you for what He has for you.

What do you feel you need to let go of in order to find your greater purpose?

Who is in your circle as a whole, and why?

Who is in your inner circle (those who you deal very closely with), and why?

Do you feel God telling you that you need to remove certain people from your life?

What does your personal time with God look like? Are there any changes you need to make to make it better?

We've talked about the importance of our words. What are you currently saying about your situation? Is there anything you need to change? Allow God to minister to you in this area.

7

Hope For Tomorrow

"I will give you back what you lost to the swarming locusts, the hopping locusts, the stripping locusts, and the cutting locusts." Joel 2:25

We've discussed a lot of things that were heavy in topic, but I wanted to end this book with hope. What does hope look like for you? For me, hope looks like Joel 2:25.

I never paid much attention to this verse until I was reading *Prophetic Reset: 40 Days to Aligning with God's Plan for Your Life* by *Joshua Giles*[5]. Page 29 discusses this verse as it relates to restoration, but it has been a verse of hope for me during this time, which is why I decided to begin this chapter with this verse. Sometimes we don't feel worthy, or important enough, to even consider that God has better in store for us. But this verse gives me hope. There is much hope to gain when you think about what was lost and the ability to recover it. This can mean not only physical possessions, but time, or dreams and aspirations that maybe were put on hold as you were trying to make your marriage work, make the other person happy, etc.

Lets go back to this verse, "I will give you back what you lost to the swarming locusts, the hopping locusts, the stripping locusts, and the cutting locusts." (Joel 2:25)

What is a locust? Simply put, a locust is a type of insect that causes destruction to plants. To a farmer destruction to their plants can cause a loss in wages and provision. I'm certainly not a farmer, nor do I understand what goes into that, but to me the locust represents the enemy (the devil) that comes to steal what is mine. He is always lurking around just trying to take something away or cause delay. 1 Peter 5:8 says, "Stay alert! Watch out for your great enemy, the devil. He prowls around like a roaring lion, looking for someone to devour." John 10:10 says, "The thief's purpose is to steal, and kill and destroy. My purpose is to give them a rich and satisfying life." Recently, I was lying in bed praying and speaking positive declarations over my life when something flew onto my arm. I jumped up out of bed so fast (because those who know me know I do not like bugs) and turned on the light. I looked around for what flew on my arm, and then I saw a creature I had never seen before. So now that I'm aware of the term locust, I said to myself "could that be a locust?" So, I looked for a picture of a locust on the internet and sure enough that's what it resembled. I believe that God sent me that locust as a sign, a covenant, that He has heard my prayers and seen my tears, and He was telling me He was going to restore me! This gave me so much hope! God heard me and loved me so much that he sent a locust to my room. A locust!!!!!!! Now you may think that was a fluke or a stroke of coincidence, but how many times have you seen a locust? I have never seen one until then…in my bedroom at that! Not only that, locusts travel in swarms. This locust was all by itself. I really believe this was just used as a sign from God for me, and in times of doubt I will remember this sign from God.

I've tried putting into words what this journey has been like for me, but the truth is there is just so much I couldn't put into words. All I know is my heart feels like a sea- large and vast- just full of emotions, desires, visions, and dreams. I'm grateful that this particular sea doesn't represent the hurt anymore, only hope.

What are you trusting God for? What do you need God to do on your behalf? God is there ready to listen to what you have to say. He wants you to know that He loves you and wants the best for you. He also wants you to know that although you have been through a tough season, He will restore you and give you back everything you have lost. You don't have to live in the past, nor let your past define you. And you don't have to settle for less than you deserve. Do not be afraid of the future or moving forward alone. God will provide. He has been my father, husband, comforter, keeper, provider, best friend and confidant......He has been my *EVERYTHING*. And I have not lacked one single day! Put your trust in Him, and He will take care of you!

Prayer

Dear God. I thank you for being God. I repent and ask forgiveness for anything I have done wrong and for getting out of alignment with your Will in any way. Please show me what areas I need to change, or make amends. Show me how I can be better. Help me to grow in you and allow you to direct my steps. I give my situation and my heart to you, and I ask for you to heal me in the areas where I hurt. Help me to forgive those who have hurt me so there will be nothing hindering me from moving forward in you. Show me your love. In Jesus name, Amen.

I encourage you to take your time as you go through the **_Self-Reflection Journal_**, ask the Holy Spirit to guide you and reveal to you what He wants you to know.

<u>Self-Reflection Journal</u>

What are you trusting God for? What do you need God to do on your behalf?

What has God shown you so far from reading this book? How will you put it to action?

Ask God to show you what He has planned for your future.

About the Author

Dr. Monica Tillett, PT, DPT

Dr. Monica Tillett is a Doctor of Physical Therapy, and has been practicing for over 16 years with a focus in geriatrics. She received her Bachelor of Science degree from Elizabeth City State University, a Master of Physical Therapy degree from Winston Salem State University, and a Doctor of Physical Therapy degree from A.T. Still University. Monica knew from a young age that she wanted to be a physical therapist. She enjoys inspiring others to become a better version of themselves when others think it is not possible. It is for this reason she has enjoyed helping seniors improve physically. Her experience includes helping seniors become as physically independent as possible through her business New Direction Rehabilitation and Wellness, Incorporated. She has also worked for other rehabilitation companies, including travel therapy companies, helping seniors in long-term care, assisted living, and other types of retirement communities.

Writing was a passion as a young child, and she has recently decided to revive this passion. Be on the lookout for more books!

References

[1] Hasa. (2016, July 14). *Difference between values and beliefs*. Pediaa.Com. https://pediaa.com/difference-between-values-and-beliefs/

[2] *Grief.com – The Five Stages of Grief*^{TM}. (n.d.-b). https://grief.com/the-five-stages-of-grief/#:~:text=The%20five%20stages%2C%20denial%2C%20anger,some%20linear%20timeline%20in%20grief.

[3] Joshua Giles Ministries. (n.d). http://www.youtube.com/@JoshuaGilesMinistries. Side note, there is another man with the same name so make sure in Google you type in https://www.joshuagiles.com, or Joshua Giles Ministries. I would point you to a specific teaching, but he has taught on restoration in so many of his teachings that I can't point to a specific one.

[4] Giles, Joshua. *Prophetic Reset: 40 Days to Aligning with God's Plan for Your Life*, pages 199-202. Minneapolis, Minnesota, Chosen Books, 2024.

[5] Giles, Joshua. *Prophetic Reset: 40 Days to Aligning with God's Plan for Your Life*, page 29. Minneapolis, Minnesota, Chosen Books, 2024.